Animals vs. Humans

MOSQUITOES INFECT

Catherine L. Osornio

WWW.APEXEDITIONS.COM

Apex is distributed by North Star Editions:
sales@northstareditions.com | 888-417-0195

Produced for Apex by Red Line Editorial.

Photographs ©: iStockphoto, cover, 1, 20–21, 42–43; Shutterstock Images, 4–5, 6–7, 8–9, 10–11, 14–15, 16–17, 18–19, 24–25, 27, 28–29, 30–31, 34–35, 36–37, 39, 40–41, 44–45, 46–47, 48–49, 50–51, 54–55, 56–57; Hulton Archive/Getty Images, 12–13; Paul Ikome/Xinhua/Alamy, 22–23; Silvia Izquierdo/AP Images, 32–33; Horst Faas/AP Image, 52–53; Red Line Editorial, 58–59

Library of Congress Control Number: 2023922209

ISBN
979-8-89250-210-8 (hardcover)
979-8-89250-231-3 (paperback)
979-8-89250-272-6 (ebook pdf)
979-8-89250-252-8 (hosted ebook)

Printed in the United States of America
Mankato, MN
082024

NOTE TO PARENTS AND EDUCATORS

Apex books are designed to build literacy skills in striving readers. Exciting, high-interest content attracts and holds readers' attention. The text is carefully leveled to allow students to achieve success quickly.

TABLE OF CONTENTS

Northern house mosquitoes are found around the world. They can spread many types of diseases.

Chapter 1

FROM BITE TO ILLNESS

A student walks by a swamp. An infected mosquito waits on the water. Suddenly, the mosquito zooms up. It lands on the student's arm. He slaps it away. But he's too late. The mosquito has bitten him.

A few days later, the student feels sick. His head and body hurt. He has a fever. So, he goes to the doctor. The doctor takes a blood test. The student has a virus. He goes home to rest. Soon, he will feel better.

Mosquitoes can lay up to 200 eggs at a time.

WATERY HOMES

Mosquitoes lay eggs in water. Some lay eggs in rivers or streams. But most mosquitoes lay eggs in still water. Ponds and swamps are common spots. So are rain-filled buckets and flowerpots.

Chapter 2

MOSQUITO PROBLEMS

Mosquitoes are flying bugs. They use their long, thin mouths to eat. Male mosquitoes eat sugar from plants. But female mosquitoes need blood. Blood helps their eggs grow. So, female mosquitoes bite other living things. Their mouths poke through skin.

More than 3,500 kinds of mosquitoes exist around the world.

Mosquitoes stick their needle-like mouths into animal or human skin.

Mosquito bites can spread sickness. First, female mosquitoes bite sick animals or people. The sickness infects the mosquitoes. Then they bite another person or animal. This spreads the sickness to others. Some illnesses spread by mosquitoes are deadly. Each year, about a million people die from mosquito illnesses.

For years, humans did not know that mosquitoes spread disease. Many people thought air was the problem. When sickness spread, people fled the area. But some scientists had a different idea. They ran tests. In 1898, one scientist showed that mosquitoes can spread sickness to birds. Two years later, another scientist learned more. He found that mosquitoes can spread sickness to humans, too.

BAD AIR

The land around Rome, Italy, is swampy. Many people got sick there in the 1800s. Italians called the disease *malaria*. That word means "bad air" in Italian. Later, people learned the truth. Malaria came from mosquitoes, not air.

Dr. Ronald Ross showed how mosquitoes spread diseases to birds. He won an award for his work.

Over time, humans fought the problem. Scientists created vaccines for some diseases. They also reduced the number of mosquitoes in certain areas. But mosquito illnesses are still common. Mosquitoes live in many swamps and jungles. They thrive in watery rice fields, too. And they continue to spread diseases around the world.

HOSPITAL TROUBLE

Mosquito illnesses are worse in poor areas. These places may not have enough hospitals or doctors. In the early 2020s, several African countries faced this problem. Those countries had the highest rates of deaths from malaria.

Brazil has large rainforests and swamps. The country has more mosquitoes than any other country.

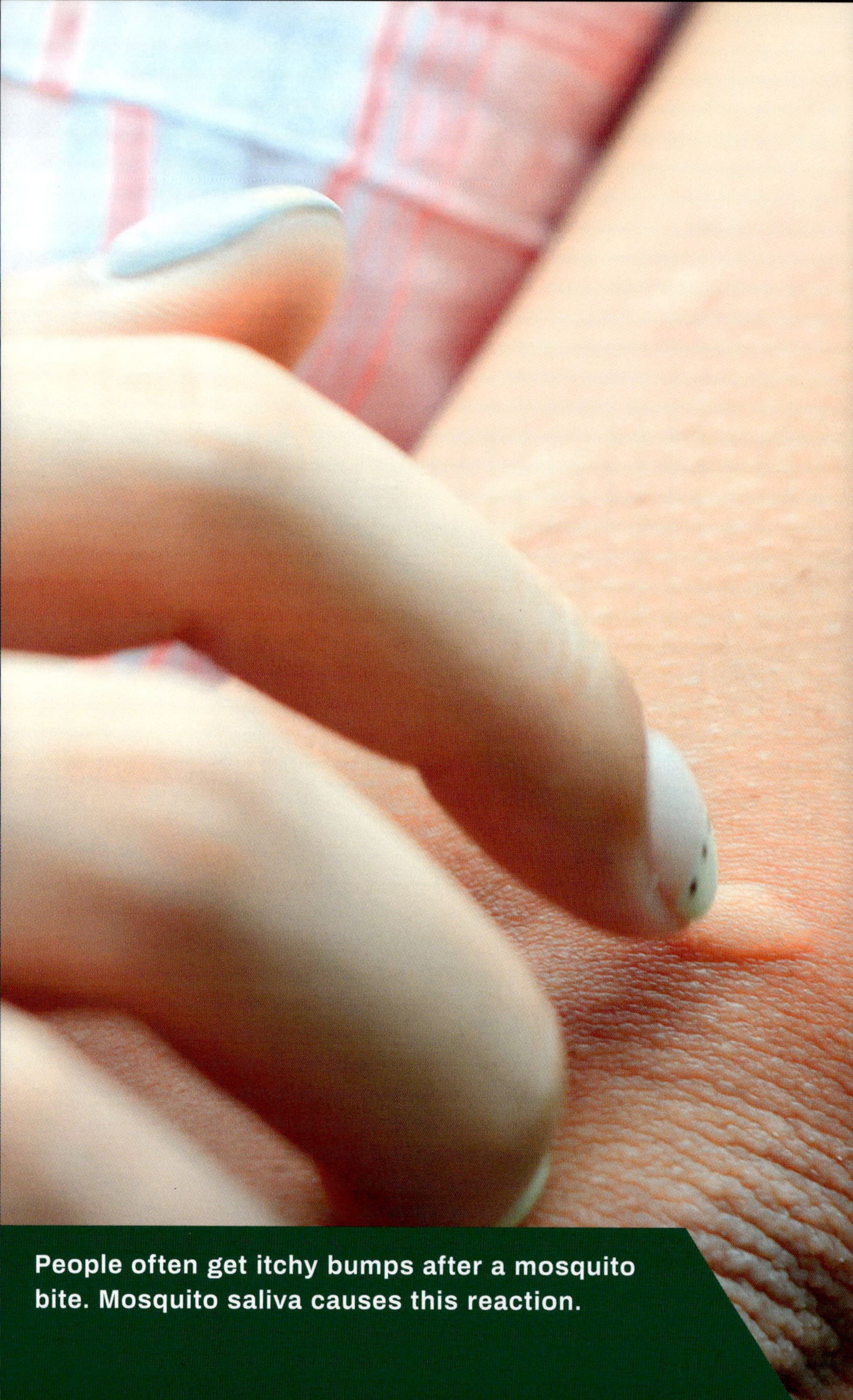

People often get itchy bumps after a mosquito bite. Mosquito saliva causes this reaction.

Chapter 3

SPREADING PARASITES

Mosquito bites leave saliva behind. The saliva can include tiny parasites. These parasites enter a person's body. Many parasites are harmful. For example, one may slow the blood flowing to the brain. It can also slow the air going to the heart.

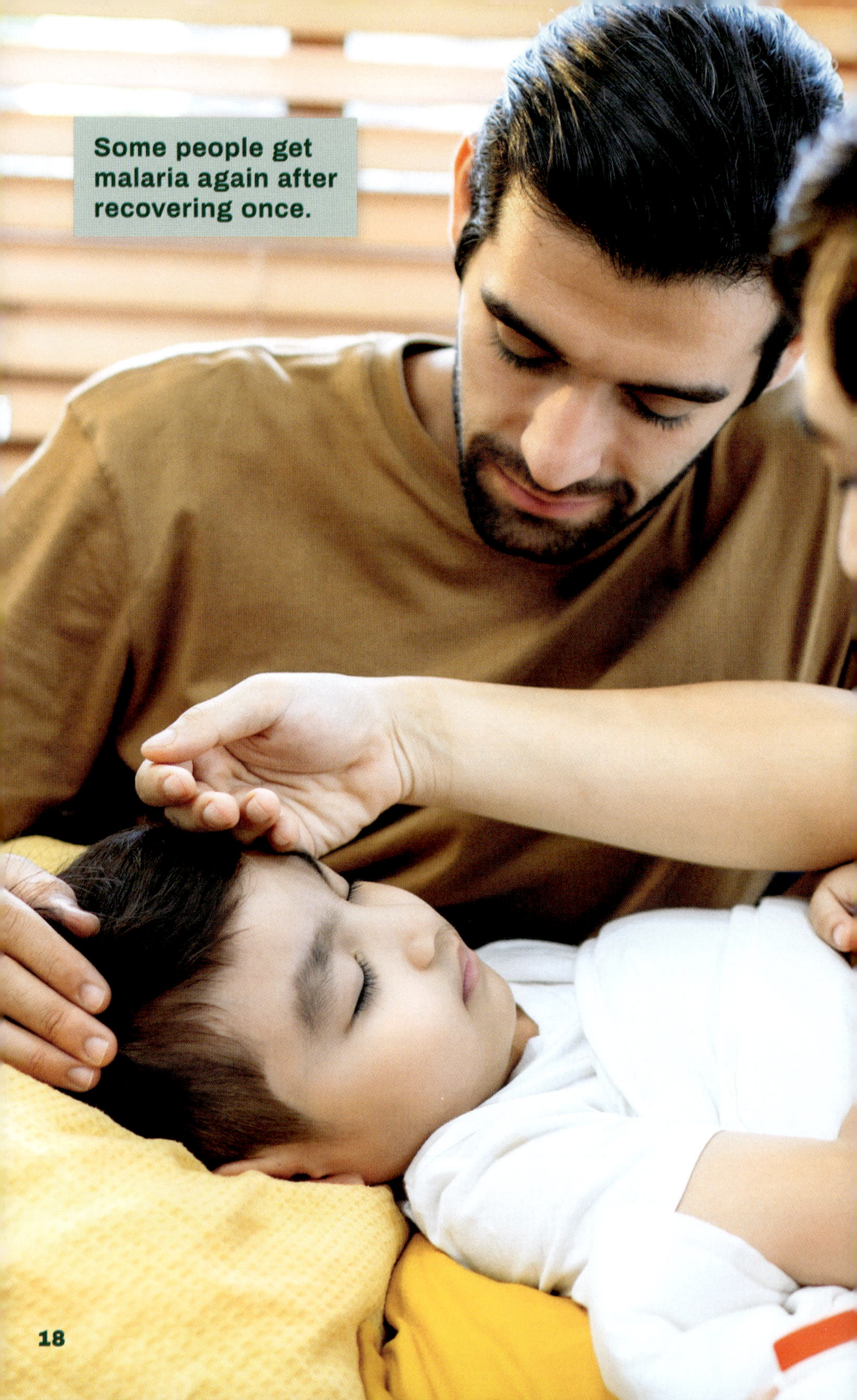

Some people get malaria again after recovering once.

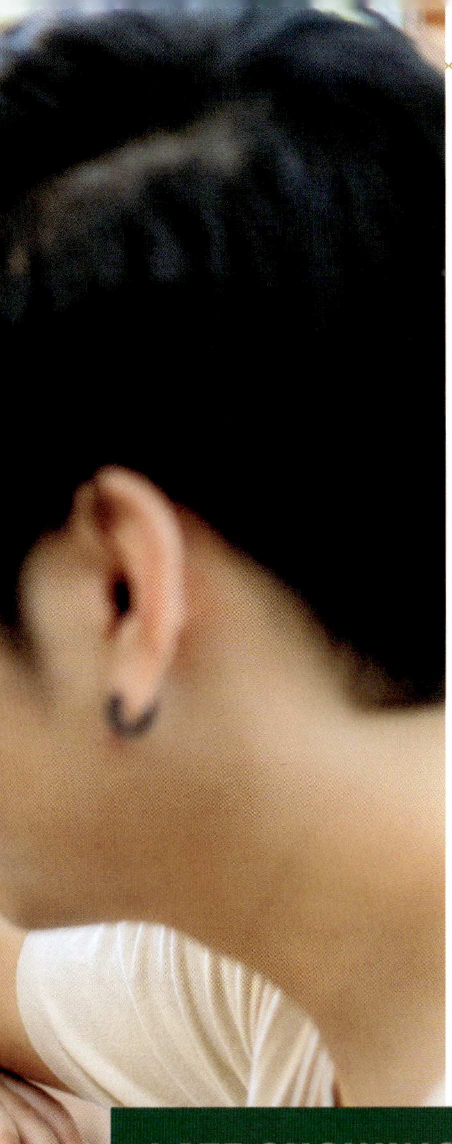

Mosquito parasites cause malaria. People with malaria get high fevers. They may feel chills and head pain. Most people get better. But young or weak people have a harder time. Their bodies struggle to fight the disease. In some areas, children make up nearly 80 percent of malaria deaths.

LATE SHOWING

Malaria symptoms don't show up right away. They appear about 10 days after the bite. So, sick people may not know they have malaria. They may travel. Mosquitoes in the new areas bite the sick people. Then malaria spreads even farther.

Malaria is common in tropical and sub-tropical areas. The wetness in these areas helps mosquitoes grow. It also helps them live longer. Nigeria is a tropical country. Mosquitoes there increase after high rainfall. They spend their lives biting humans. It is hard for people there to control the spread.

SMELLING A TARGET

Mosquitoes can smell a person's breath. They can also smell the soap on people's skin. Mosquitoes can even smell blood type. Some mosquitoes target people with type O blood.

Nigeria has a higher death rate for malaria than any other country.

In January 2024, the first malaria vaccine program began. It happened in Cameroon.

Sometimes, human actions spread malaria. That situation happened during World War II (1939–1945). German soldiers flooded the land around Rome. They wanted to slow down the enemy. The extra water made the land swampier. That caused mosquitoes to grow in number. Thousands of people got malaria.

A NEW METHOD

Many medicines help treat malaria. In the 1980s, people started work on a vaccine. But malaria parasites are complicated. The process was hard. The vaccine was finally ready in 2021.

Sometimes, people with lymphatic filariasis can't work or move well. Living with the disease can be hard.

Mosquitoes carry other parasites, too. Some carry tiny worms. These worms cause many diseases. Lymphatic filariasis is one painful disease. The disease causes liquids to build up. Body parts swell. It can even disable people.

LIVING WITH PAIN

People can treat some worm diseases. Medicines kill the worms. But often, people in poor areas can't get the medicines. They have to live with the diseases.

That's Wild!

WINNING A WAR

Mosquitoes played a role in the American Revolutionary War (1775–1783). In 1781, British soldiers marched north. They headed to Yorktown, Virginia. The area was swampy. Mosquitoes with malaria lived there.

Many American soldiers could resist malaria. They had been sick before. But the British soldiers were not immune. Many of these soldiers were already weak. Then they reached Yorktown. Thousands fell ill with malaria. Soon, more than 60 percent were too sick to fight. In October 1781, the British army had to quit. They surrendered.

In the 2020s, areas around Yorktown were still swampy.

Chapter 4

SPREADING VIRUSES

Some kinds of mosquitoes carry viruses. Mosquitoes spread viruses the same way they spread parasites. Infected mosquitoes bite. That puts the viruses into other living things. Some of these viruses are well known. They have harmed humans for centuries.

A mosquito may bite five or six times before it is full.

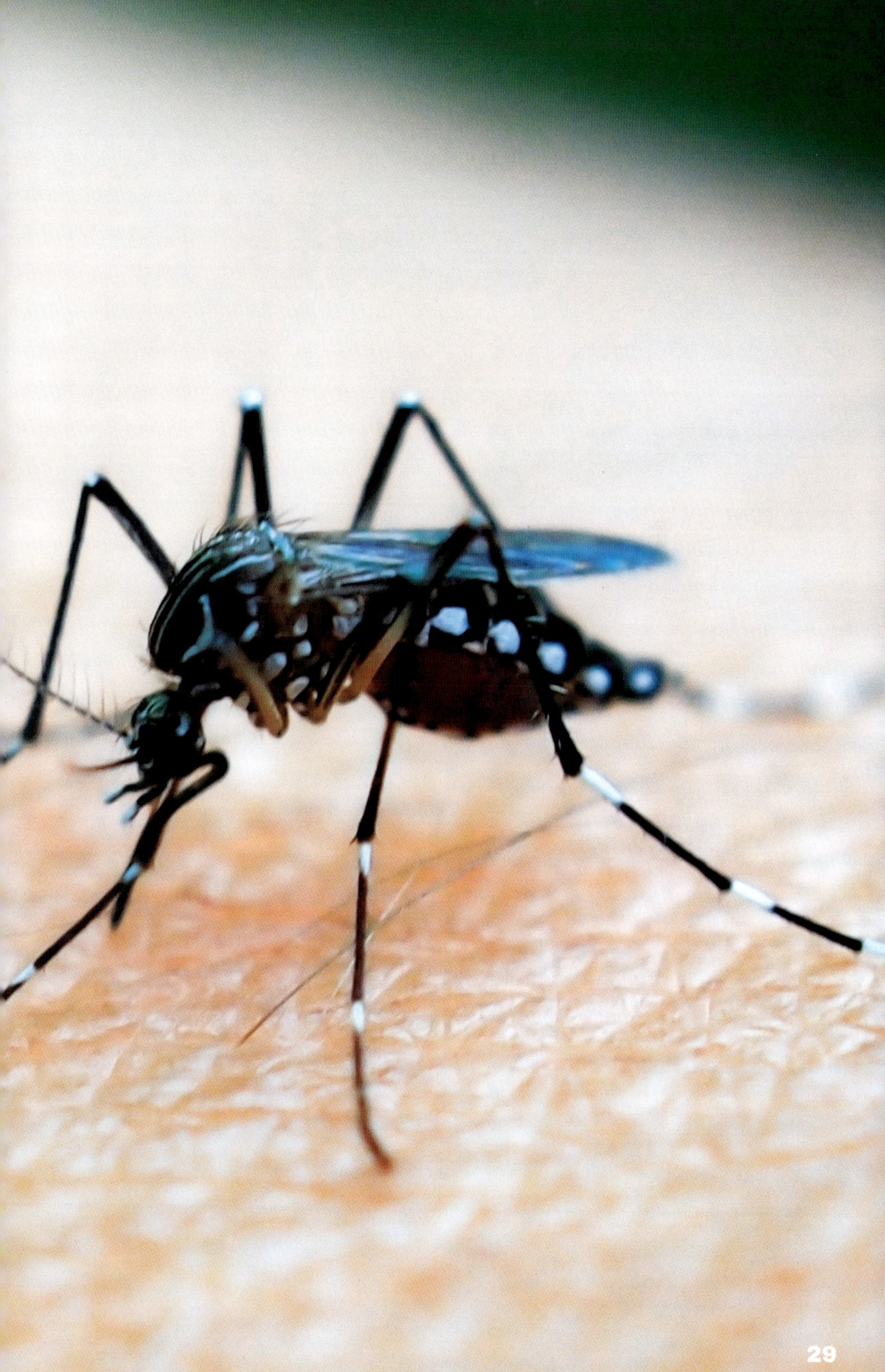

Dengue fever is caused by a virus. It is most common in Southeast Asia. The disease can be mild. Most people don't show symptoms. But sometimes it leads to fevers, pain, and rashes. Other cases are more serious. People throw up. They feel weak and thirsty. Dengue can even cause death.

BREAKBONE

Dengue fever is also called "breakbone fever." The illness brings strong pain. Some people say it feels like their bones are breaking.

Asian tiger mosquitoes spread dengue viruses.

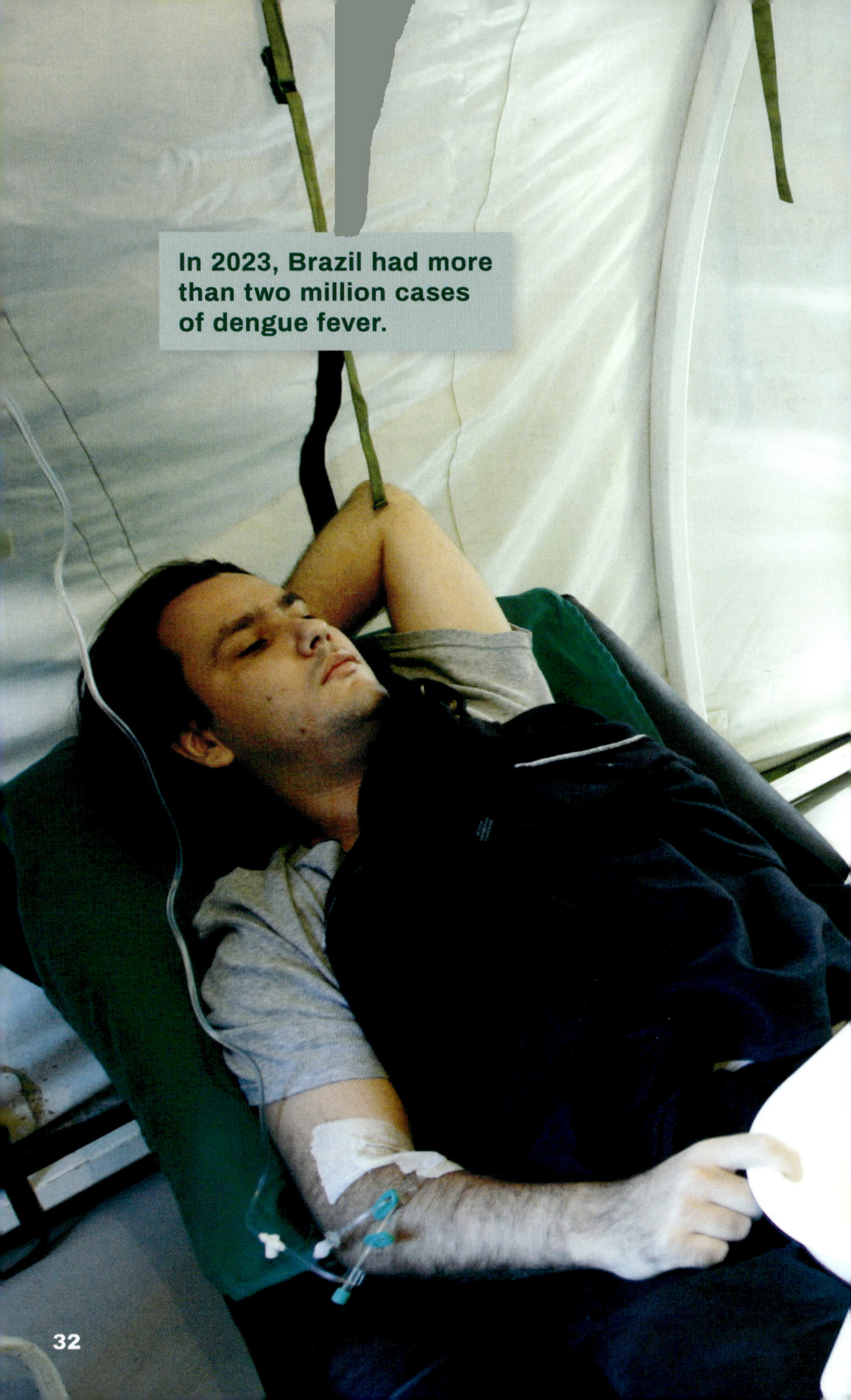

In 2023, Brazil had more than two million cases of dengue fever.

Millions of people get sick with dengue each year. In 2023, more than 100 countries had cases of dengue. But there is no cure. People can only take pain medicine. They must wait for the disease to pass.

The eyes of yellow fever patients may turn yellow.

Another common mosquito virus is yellow fever. Around 200,000 cases happen each year. After infection, people get fevers, head pain, and chills. Yellow fever attacks the liver, too. As the disease gets worse, skin turns yellow. In some cases, vomit is black.

BLACK VOMIT

People call yellow fever different names. Some call the disease "yellow jack." In Spanish, some people called it *vomito negro*. That means black vomit.

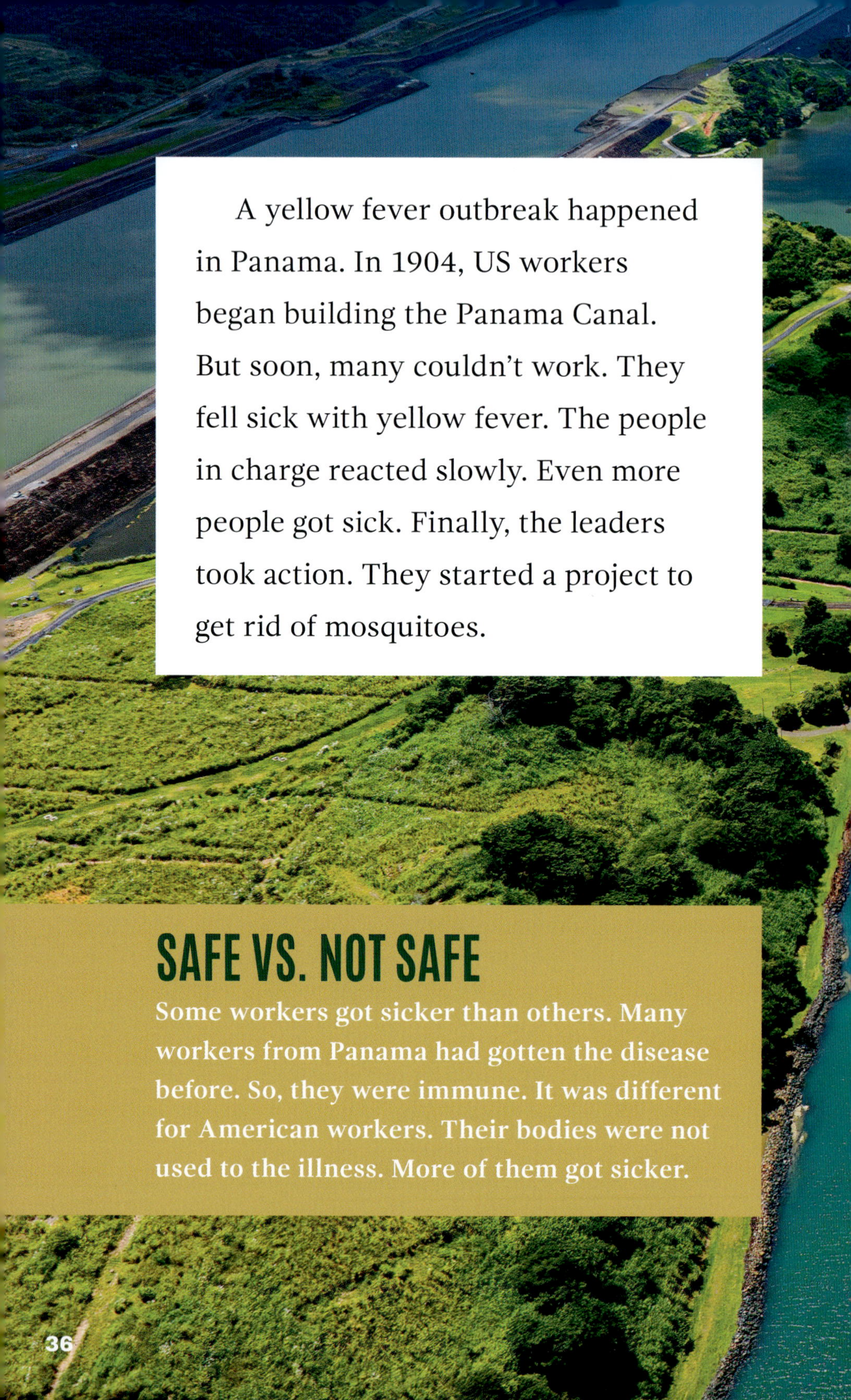

A yellow fever outbreak happened in Panama. In 1904, US workers began building the Panama Canal. But soon, many couldn't work. They fell sick with yellow fever. The people in charge reacted slowly. Even more people got sick. Finally, the leaders took action. They started a project to get rid of mosquitoes.

SAFE VS. NOT SAFE

Some workers got sicker than others. Many workers from Panama had gotten the disease before. So, they were immune. It was different for American workers. Their bodies were not used to the illness. More of them got sicker.

The Panama Canal connects the Pacific and Atlantic Oceans. It took 10 years to build.

That's Wild!

CLEANING PANAMA

William Gorgas was an American army doctor. He had experience getting rid of yellow fever. So, during the outbreak at the Panama Canal, leaders had an idea. They called Gorgas. He went to Panama. His team got to work.

Jars and cups lay on the streets. These collected water. Gorgas's team cleaned up all this trash. They covered water buckets. They added faucets to closed containers. Their actions worked. Soon, fewer mosquitoes lived in the area. Workers could finish the canal.

William Gorgas's team sprayed chemicals around the canal. People still do this in some areas.

Chapter 5

MORE MOSQUITO VIRUSES

Over time, humans faced even more mosquito viruses. In 1931, people discovered Japanese encephalitis. Most people with this virus don't show signs. But some cases harm the brain. Sick people may fall into comas. They may have seizures. One in four people die.

When someone is in a coma, they are unconscious for a long time.

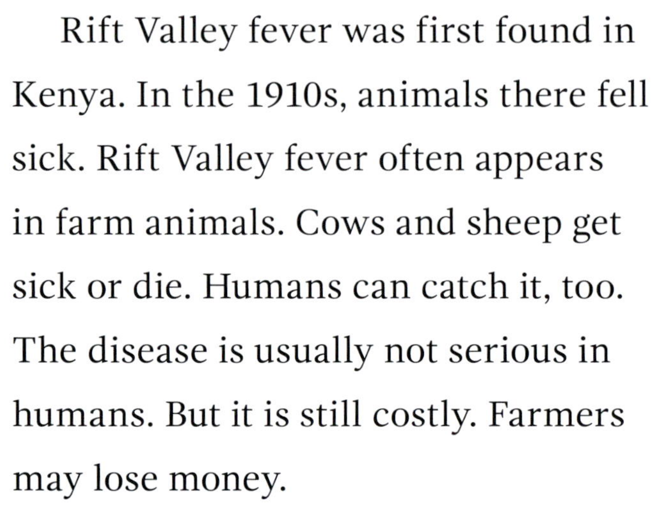

Rift Valley fever was first found in Kenya. In the 1910s, animals there fell sick. Rift Valley fever often appears in farm animals. Cows and sheep get sick or die. Humans can catch it, too. The disease is usually not serious in humans. But it is still costly. Farmers may lose money.

EAT UP

Many animals eat mosquitoes. Bats and beetles may eat them. Fish eat mosquito eggs. These animals can't get rid of all mosquitoes. But they can help control the number.

Other insects such as dragonflies eat mosquitoes.

West Nile virus came to the United States in 1999. It is often spread through birds.

Another mosquito virus is West Nile virus. It was first noticed in Uganda in 1937. Now, it is the most common mosquito disease in the United States. West Nile often affects birds, horses, and other animals. But it can also reach humans. Most people do not have symptoms. But sometimes, people get fevers and feel numb. In some cases, they may die.

Mosquitoes also spread Zika virus. Zika often comes and goes without harm. But the disease is dangerous for babies. Sometimes, Zika infects pregnant women. The infection can harm the babies. Their babies can develop brain problems.

NEW FINDS

People are still discovering new kinds of mosquitoes. Some of these mosquitoes have moved into new areas. They may grow in number. They can even take over the mosquitoes that already lived there. This can carry disease to new places.

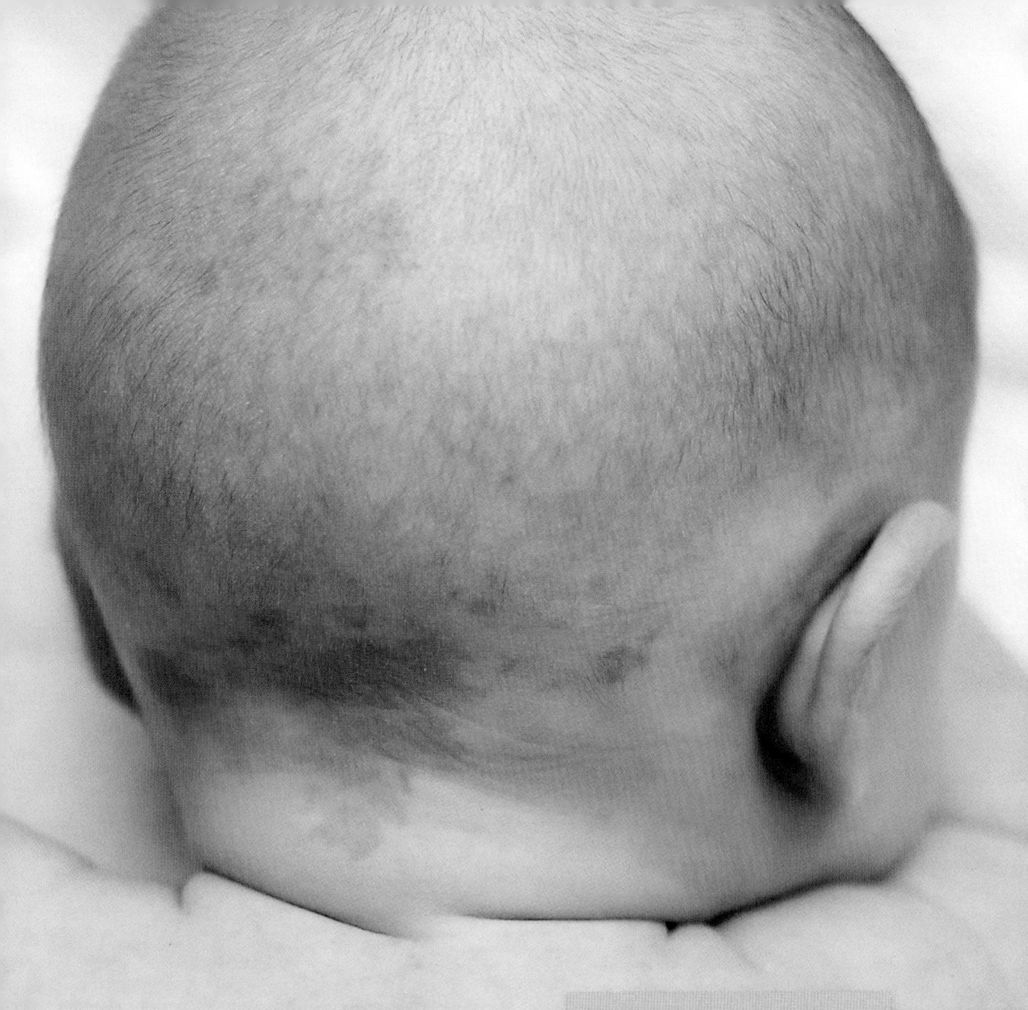

People with Zika may have a fever, rash, and pain.

People can't spread the chikungunya virus to other humans. Only mosquitoes can give someone the virus.

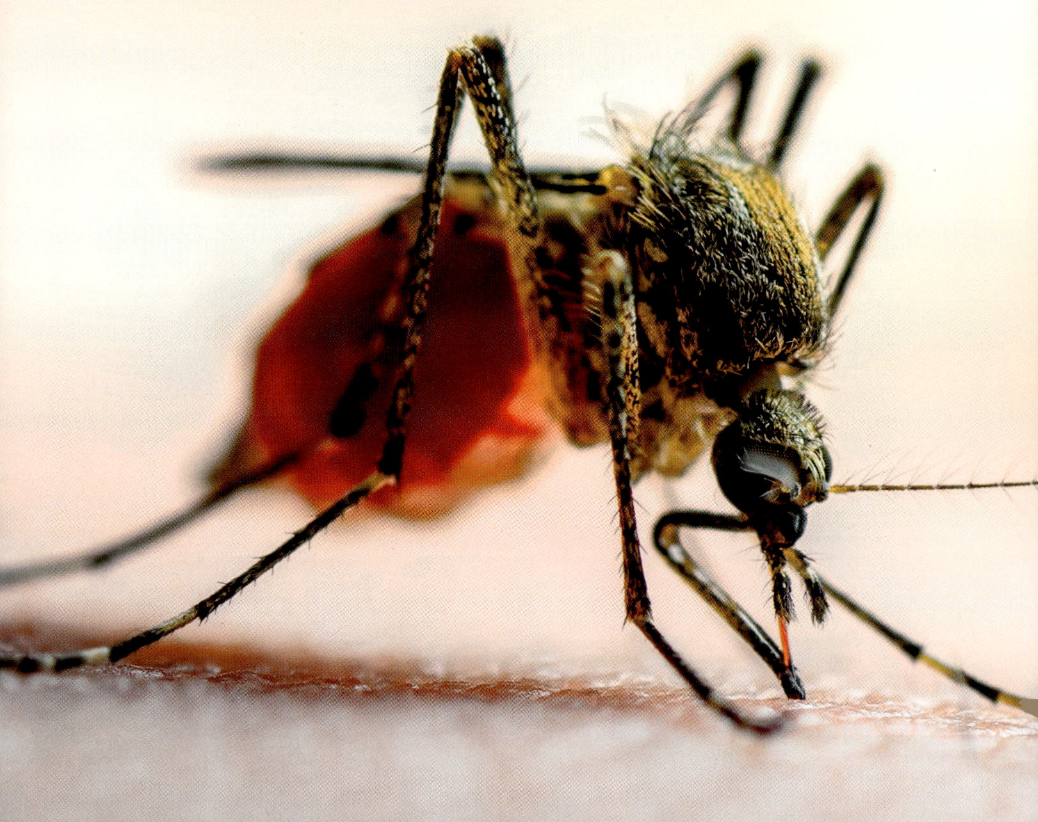

Humans discovered the chikungunya virus in the 1950s. It was found in Tanzania. Then chikungunya spread to many countries. Sick people feel terrible body pain. They might walk stiffly or stoop over. But after a week, people usually feel better.

LOOKING DEEPER

In the 1820s, better microscopes helped scientists learn more about germs. They found a link to mosquitoes. This helped scientists track diseases. And doctors could treat them better.

Chapter 6

CONTROLLING THE PROBLEM

Humans have found many ways to treat mosquito illnesses. Medicines have helped. But stopping sickness from happening is best. That way, people don't get sick in the first place. Vaccines are one method. Limiting the number of mosquitoes also helps.

Malaria vaccines help reduce deaths from malaria.

Bug sprays are a common way to fight mosquitoes. Some sprays kill adult mosquitoes. Others target eggs. Farmers spray large areas of land. People can buy sprays for personal use, too. Many people put bug spray on their bodies. Then they go outside. Most mosquitoes stay away. They don't try to bite.

A HISTORIC SPRAY

Mosquitoes made many people sick during World War II. So, Americans created a powerful spray called DDT. The chemical hurt nature. The United States banned it. But as of the early 2020s, some countries still used it.

Insects feed on animals and plants. Many farmers used DDT to kill the insects.

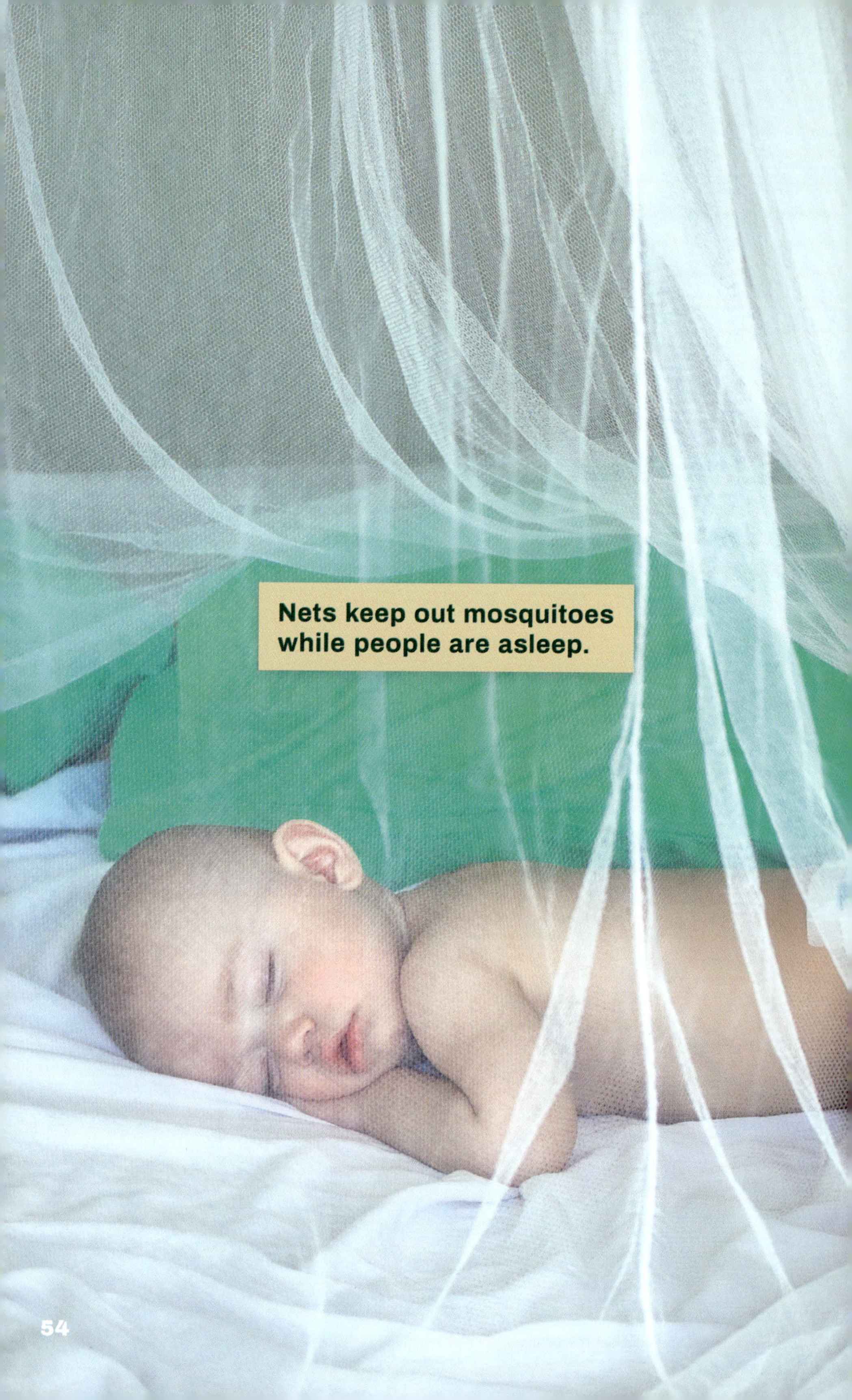

Nets keep out mosquitoes while people are asleep.

Making changes to an area can reduce the number of mosquitoes. After rainstorms, many outdoor items fill up with water. Pots, old tires, and buckets are some examples. Mosquito eggs can grow there. People should dump them out. Using nets helps, too. Nets can go over windows. They can cover beds. That way, mosquitoes can't get in to bite.

COVERING UP

Mosquitoes must reach skin to bite. So, clothing can protect against mosquitoes. Long sleeves and pants help people cover up. Mosquitoes can get close. But they can't bite.

Humans take many actions to stay safe from mosquitoes. But the problem is still huge. In the early 2020s, companies and scientists were still working to fix things. They wanted to get more medicines to people. And they were working on new ways to keep people safe.

Mosquito sprays can kill bees, other important insects, and pets.

HURTING NATURE

Some methods of decreasing mosquito numbers can hurt nature. For example, some bug sprays make other animals sick. And some living things need mosquitoes to eat. New methods try to keep humans and nature safe.

MAP

1. Panama Canal, Panama: Mosquitoes spread yellow fever and malaria among workers building the Panama Canal.
2. Yorktown, Virginia: British soldiers fall sick with malaria, leading to their surrender in the Revolutionary War.

3. Rome, Italy: Mosquitoes infect people with malaria after German soldiers flood the area during World War II.

4. Uganda: Scientists discover mosquitoes carrying West Nile virus.

5. Kenya: Farm animals fall sick with Rift Valley fever.

6. Southeast Asia: Hot and wet land leads to more mosquitoes and mosquito illnesses.

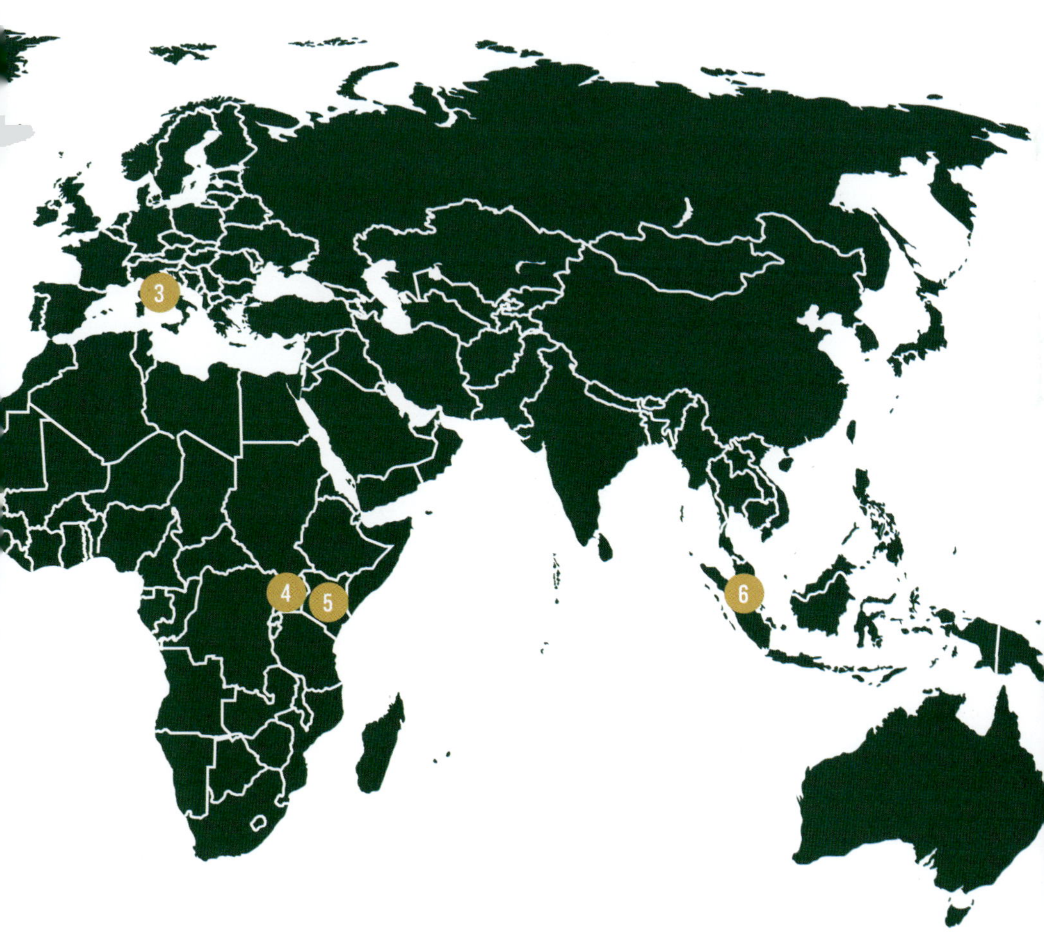

COMPREHENSION QUESTIONS

Write your answers on a separate piece of paper.

1. Write a few sentences to explain where mosquitoes live.

2. Which mosquito illness do you think is the worst? Why?

3. Which illness is caused by a mosquito parasite?

   A. Japanese encephalitis
   B. dengue fever
   C. malaria

4. Why might farmers lose money if their animals catch Rift Valley fever?

   A. Sick animals may get stronger after recovering.
   B. Sick animals may work slowly or die.
   C. Sick animals may attack farmers.

5. What does **mild** mean in this book?

*The disease can be **mild**. Most people don't show symptoms. But sometimes it leads to fevers, pain, and rashes.*

A. deadly
B. not strong
C. hard to spread

6. What does **surrendered** mean in this book?

*Soon, more than 60 percent were too sick to fight. In October 1781, the British army had to quit. They **surrendered**.*

A. started fighting
B. gave up
C. asked for more soldiers

Answer key on page 64.

GLOSSARY

disable
To cause limits or differences in a person's senses or movements.

immune
Protected from sickness because the body is no longer affected by it.

infected
Filled with germs that cause a disease.

microscopes
Tools that make very small things look bigger.

parasites
Organisms that can grow in the body and cause sickness.

seizures
Changes in the brain that cause shaking or other problems.

swamp
An area of low land covered in water, often with many plants.

symptoms
Signs of an illness or disease.

tropical
Having weather that is often warm and wet.

vaccines
Substances that help a person's body fight a disease.

virus
A tiny substance that can cause illness in people and animals.

TO LEARN MORE

BOOKS

Murray, Julie. *Mosquitoes.* Minneapolis: Abdo Publishing, 2020.

Pallotta, Jerry. *Blue Whale vs. Mosquito.* New York: Scholastic, 2024.

Peterson, Megan Cooley. *Dangerous Bugs: Mosquitoes.* Mankato, MN: Black Rabbit Books, 2024.

ONLINE RESOURCES

Visit **www.apexeditions.com** to find links and resources related to this title.

ABOUT THE AUTHOR

Catherine L. Osornio has been writing for children since 2003. She lives with her family in Southern California. When not writing, Catherine likes to read children's books, draw cartoons, and work in her garden.

INDEX

ANSWER KEY:

1. Answers will vary; 2. Answers will vary; 3. C; 4. B; 5. B; 6. B